AN AUGMENTED REALITY
SCIENCE EXPERIENCE

CURIOUS PEARL
SCIENCE GIRL

CURIOUS PEARL
OBSERVES MIGRATION

by Eric Braun

illustrated by Stephanie Dehennin

raintree

a Capstone company — publishers for children

Curious Pearl here! Do you like science? I certainly do! I have all sorts of fun tools to help me observe and investigate, but my favourite tool is my science notebook. That's where I write down questions and facts that help me learn more about science. Would you like to join me on my science adventures? You're in for a special surprise!

Download the Capstone 4D app!

Videos for all of the notebook features in this book are at your fingertips with the 4D app.

To download the Capstone 4D app:

- Search in the Apple App Store or Google Play for "Capstone 4D"
- Click Install (Android) or Get, then Install (Apple)
- Open the application
- Scan any page with this icon

You can also access the additional resources on the web at www.capstone4D.com using the password **pearl.migration**

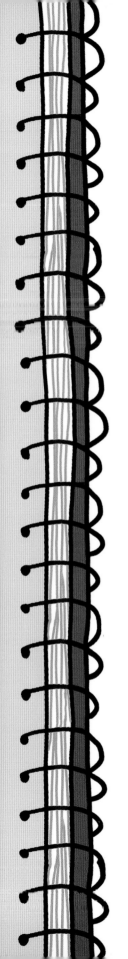

Saturdays are "Sal days". I always visit my friend Sal.

"Hi Sal!" I said. "What's wrong?"

"All summer long, pretty little birds called warblers were nesting in my garden," he said. "But now they're gone. Maybe I scared them."

"It's autumn," I said. "Maybe they've gone back to school." I nudged him with my elbow and giggled to myself.

But Sal was not in the mood for jokes.

"Sorry," I said. "I'm sure they didn't leave because of you. Let's see if we can solve this mystery." I pulled out my notebook and pencil.

"We'll never work it out," replied Sal.

"Come on, Sal. Let's try!" I said.

4

"OK," said Sal. "I'm in. What should we do?"

"Well, what would a scientist do?" I asked.

"Observe!" answered Sal.

"Eureka!" I said. That's a super scientific word! I use it when I'm excited about discovering something new. "Let's go!"

We headed off to the woods to learn about animal behaviour.

"Look at those squirrels," said Sal.

"They're collecting seeds and acorns," I replied. "They need food for the winter."

"And those beavers are building a lodge in the stream," said Sal. "They need a safe place to live."

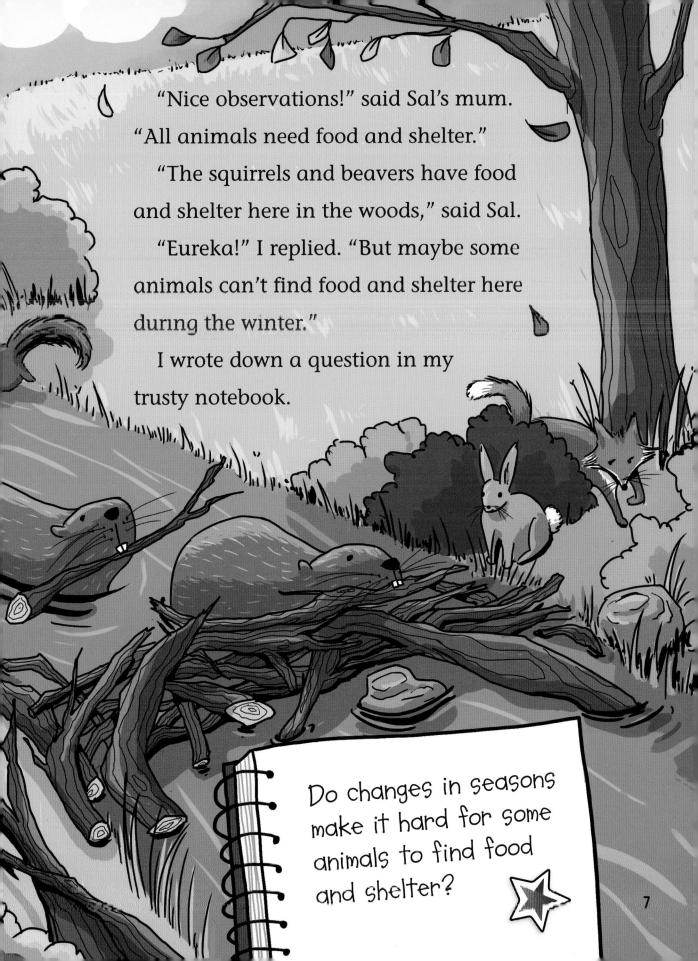

"Nice observations!" said Sal's mum. "All animals need food and shelter."

"The squirrels and beavers have food and shelter here in the woods," said Sal.

"Eureka!" I replied. "But maybe some animals can't find food and shelter here during the winter."

I wrote down a question in my trusty notebook.

Do changes in seasons make it hard for some animals to find food and shelter?

We headed back to Sal's house and sat down on the patio.

"So where do warblers find shelter?" I asked.

"They used to hang around in those bushes," Sal said. "Before they got angry with me and left."

"Don't be silly," I said. "They didn't get angry. Look! The bushes are losing their leaves. Winter is coming!"

"Can you see those goldfinches?" I asked. "Did the warblers like your bird feeder too?"

"No," Sal said. "They eat insects. They find them in the bushes where they nest."

"Eureka!" I said. "Bugs are like leaves. They are harder to find in the winter."

"Just like yellow warblers," Sal said.

I opened my notebook and wrote down another question.

How do animals find shelter and food in winter?

9

"What else happens in the winter?" I asked Sal.

"The football season!" he said.

"No!" I said. "I'm talking about the weather."

"Oh, you mean it gets cold," he said. "And the sweet little yellow warblers go away."

"Eureka! It gets cold." I replied. "We can put on hats and coats, but birds can't. My mum once told me that birds fluff up their feathers to stay warm."

"That makes sense, Pearl!" said Sal.

I wrote this down in my notebook.

How do birds stay warm in winter? Some birds fluff up and trap body heat in their feathers.

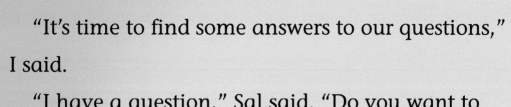

"It's time to find some answers to our questions," I said.

"I have a question," Sal said. "Do you want to play football?"

"Later," I said. "Don't you want to work out what happened to the warblers?"

"All I know is they've gone," Sal said. "And they're not coming back."

"Follow me," I told him.

Sal and I went inside. I grabbed our tablet and typed *warblers* into the search engine. It pulled up information for us.

"Look," I said. "It says here that warblers fly south in the winter. It's called migration."

I wrote down the definition of *migrate* in my notebook.

When animals migrate, they move to another area to find food and shelter.

"The warblers will come back in the spring," I said. "Then they'll find insects and live in the leafy bushes."

"Brilliant!" he said.

Sal pointed to the screen. "Look," he said. "The answer to all of your questions is to do with the weather. It says here that in Africa it stays warmer in the winter. Leaves don't fall, so warblers can safely nest in bushes. The insects eat the leaves, and warblers eat the insects."

"Eureka!" I replied. "That's it, Sal!"

"It says here that in spring it gets too hot in the south," I said. "The warblers fly north again."

"That sounds like a lot of work," Sal said. "Do all animals do that?"

"I don't know," I said.

"Salmon," said Sal's mum as she offered us a plate.

"Salmon sandwiches?" Sal asked. "Yuck!"

"No," she said. "Salmon migrate. We used to see them in a stream when I was your age. They live in the sea but swim upstream to lay eggs. The stream has fewer predators, so it's a safer place to lay eggs."

"That makes sense," I said.

I wrote down a note about salmon.

Some animals, like salmon, migrate to lay eggs or breed.

17

"It sounds like there are lots of reasons animals migrate," Sal said. "To find food. To find shelter."

"To find a safe place to breed or raise their young," Sal's mum said.

We looked up other migrating animals online. We found out that zebras travel almost 3,200 kilometres (2,000 miles) every year to find fresh grass and water!

We learnt that all sorts of animals migrate: butterflies, birds, insects, deer, snakes, sharks, bats, elephants and frogs. Geese, crabs and earthworms also migrate. Caribou migrate too. I made a note in my notebook.

Caribou migrate to find food and give birth to their young.

Sal said, "I'm glad the warblers will be back."

"In the spring," I said. "Meanwhile, will you show me how to make a bird feeder like yours?"

"Sure," he said.

"Great!" I said. "I'm excited to see what kind of birds migrate my way!"

People and Animals Migrate

1. Think of any family members or friends you know who have moved to a different place. Write down their names on a sheet of paper.

2. Ask an adult if you can call or e-mail as many of them as possible. Ask each of them to explain the reasons why they moved.

3. Make a chart that shows people's reasons for moving.

4. Ask an adult to help you research migrating animals online. Make a list of as many migrating animals as possible. Explain why the animals migrate.

5. Do people and animals migrate for the same reasons? What are some connections you notice? Tell an adult about your findings.

GLOSSARY

behaviour the way a person or animal acts

breed mate and produce young

eureka cry of joy or satisfaction

lodge beaver's home of mud, logs and sticks, built in the water

migrate move from one place to another

migration the regular movement of animals from one place to another as they search for food or resources

observation something you have noticed by watching carefully

observe to watch something closely in order to learn something

predator an animal that hunts other animals for food

shelter a place where an animal can stay safe from weather and other animals

warbler a small songbird

BOOKS

Monarch Butterfly Migration (Animal Migration), Grace Hansen (Abdo Kids Jumbo, 2017)

When Whales Cross the Sea: The Gray Whale Migration (Extraordinary Migrations), Sharon Katz Cooper (Raintree, 2015)

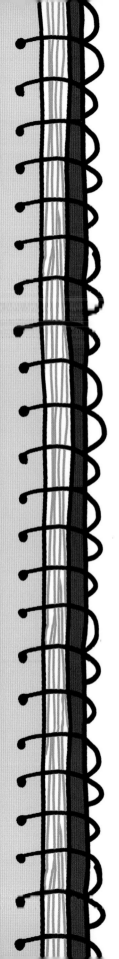

WEBSITES

https://www.rspb.org.uk/kids-and-schools/kids-and-families/kids/play/migrationmap.aspx
This site shows a map of animal migration routes.

https://ypte.org.uk/factsheets/migration/why-do-they-migrate
This site explains why animals migrate.

COMPREHENSION QUESTIONS

What are three reasons that an animal might migrate?

Some animals migrate very long distances. What are some challenges they might face on such a long journey?

Can people migrate? Why or why not? Give an example.

MORE BOOKS IN THE SERIES

INDEX

Raintree is an imprint of Capstone Global Library Limited, a company incorporated in England and Wales having its registered office at 264 Banbury Road, Oxford, OX2 7DY – Registered company number: 6695582

www.raintree.co.uk
myorders@raintree.co.uk

Text © Capstone Global Library Limited 2018
The moral rights of the proprietor have been asserted.

Edited by Shelly Lyons
Designed by Ted Williams
Art Director: Nathan Gassman
Production by Katy LaVigne
Printed and bound in China

ISBN 978 1 4747 4052 4
21 20 19 18 17
10 9 8 7 6 5 4 3 2 1

British Library Cataloguing in Publication Data
A full catalogue record for this book is available from the British Library.

Acknowledgements
We would like to thank Christopher T Ruhland, PhD, for his invaluable help in the preparation of this book.

The illustrations in this book were digitally produced.

Every effort has been made to contact copyright holders of material reproduced in this book. Any omissions will be rectified in subsequent printings if notice is given to the publisher.

All the Internet addresses (URLs) given in this book were valid at the time of going to press. However, due to the dynamic nature of the Internet, some addresses may have changed, or sites may have changed or ceased to exist since publication. While the author and publisher regret any inconvenience this may cause readers, no responsibility for any such changes can be accepted by either the author or the publisher.